# Writer For No Reason

A Collection of Inspirational Poems For
Writers All Around The Globe

Devnum Nagar

# Dedication

To all the writers who are hesitant or feel something is stopping them from opening their void like a bursting balloon waiting to explode into the cosmic air.

# Preface

"Writer For No Reason: A Collection of Inspirational Poems For Writers All Around The Globe" was born out of a mystic void. These poems are a mirror-like reflection into that void. I pray and hope for each writer reading this that they overcome this challenge of being a writer in today's world. I'm not here to tell you if the road not taken is right or wrong, I'm here to pat your back while you're at the crossroads.

# Acknowledgements

My bitchin and heartfelt thanks to the void that made me write and see the world through a completely different perspective. Some credit goes to the photographer in me. And the other to the filmmaker that is yet to burst out of me. Special thanks to my readers for bearing with me and sharing this world with me. You guys make me worthwhile, and so does this beautiful Nature. Your support and understanding are highly valued.

XOXO

# Poem 1

I lift myself each day and pat my back for no reason
I try to smile but keep this resting bitch face for no
reason
I want to help but push away for no reason
I am healing, they say, for no reason
I see through all of it for no reason
I am and will be writing every day for no reason.

# Poem 2

What do you do when writing doesn't come to you?
Do you come to it or let it come to you?
Who can really answer that? Guess? Obviously 'You.'
Days when you drop your strength a little and worry
about your survival.
Your faith declines, and almost everything seems to
move away.
Your favorite things lose their charm, do you then love
writing letters to yourself?
Does it help? Does it become your companion?
Or do you ignite it cause you have nowhere else to be?
I say it's all fate to me now.
Writing and Fate are siblings born from different
mothers.
One holds you and one teaches you how to hold and be
held.
Both travel on a road holding hands, glancing at each
other, like lovers but distant but close.
They fall far to fall close.
Sometimes, it is what they say and every time not so

much but all to make one.

It's just a day or just a night but remember it's all for you.

Not writing is also writing my fellow companion.

# Poem 3

*A wind of books sways over my head*
*I feel them, but can't seem to touch*
*They fly higher, as I try to catch them,*
*Just like two birds on a single branch*
*Tweeting their desires, but disturbed by a human.*
*They rush to fly their secrets away,*
*For once, said in the open, it might never return*
*These books keep castling themselves in my wake.*
For I know one day the wind will be sweet,
That these books will fall for me.

# Poem 4

Days when the emptiness just creeps in without any
notice,
It's those little pinpricks of time,
Stabbing you right into the void.
You feel the weight of your existence, and oh, it's heavier
each time.
But you continue to lift yourself anyway, cause it's the
only way.
Your breath is heavy and you need some peace
You know no peace will be at your feet until you write it
down
So you tell yourself, just put it down
Whatever, sun, moon and stars,
All are yours, you see them and you reflect
What you were writing, was you all along.

# Poem 5

You make me feel like all the love, I never had poured
into my bones,
Reviving me from the long dead.
You breathe life into me like I was never born,
What do I do when it's you who awakens all the love in
my soul?
I do not know a thing about life without you.

# Poem 6

*When the poetry is lethal do you call it death or a rap
battle?
Some words cut deeper than a knife but you keep going.
Death kissing you and romancing the knife to warn you
It's a rap battle of my mind and the death of my heart
that tells me to leave.
But will I give in my melancholy?
I want to come out of this body that horrifies me to see
the daylight,
Only your kiss of paper, might save my heart, my mind,
my body and my soul
Maybe then those three words would have a meaning for
a change
Poetry, poetry, poetry.*

# Poem 7

I'm a tree for your roots deeply watered and soiled
You hold me upright when I sway by the winds of desire
You preach of the flattering leaves and the color pallet
you own
I see only beauty to sit on your ground and weep my
sorrows on paper
My hands hug you to show you love that is beyond of
this world
My dear tree you get deciduous when I start to walk
away
You fail to see your pitch only for me to remind you that
you are my favorite tree.
Full of air and full of life, to me you are divine.

# Poem 8

Writing in the noise, my ears hear flutes playing behind,
I do not match or care for my words to have space
I let them spill on paper and feel the flow.
My body sways along with my fingers as I type,
It's not unbearably heavy if you love what you do.

# Poem 9

I was primarily depressed, after which I rewired my
brain,
You are not alone, the titles started to rain.
Smelly alcohol and stained bedsheets
No friends banging the door, I was alone
Notepad kept me woke as I drowned into each layer of
hope.

# Poem 10

Always a loner but a good friend,
Handwritten letters and dairy milk
I'll write sick letters to excuse you sometime,
So that you fall sick with me, besides
I'll watch you, take notes, and almost say,
What I've hidden in closed doors, maybe for you to open
and take
I'm always a little afraid, what if my fancy doesn't match
yours?
I'll keep you closest, and not say, oh, but I have to
someday.

# Poem 11

Writers earn more is the biggest lie I have ever heard
after the word illusion,
Until I saw Zoya Akhtar's Movie Trailer called
'Superboys Of Malegaon.'
Saw many movies, but never the one to move mountains
within me,
All the storms of chaos raveling inside me and falling
like dandruff on my tee.
I hated the plight, but somehow woke up to a light,
Too dark and then too bright, I wasn't me for a while
The words " Writer Baap Hota Hai" abducted my soul
I knew somewhere that something was right, even if
Kaliyuga was here to take away my stride.

# Poem 12

No reason, I am often exhausted,
Similar screens and faces bombarded.
I wish to run away into a deep forest, find a cottage with
people who could adopt me and love me forever.
I wish to stay within the community, knit scarfs, talk
with animals, braid my hair with beautiful flowers, make
garlands, wear pastel gowns, do daily chores, read books,
secretly find passages to magical pathways, meet the
love of my life and go on evening strolls hand in hand
cherishing the little things in life.
I wish to write under a tree with some sandwiches,
quenching my ravenous hunger.
I see reason and then not, it keeps switching like a
flickering light bulb in the cottage. I choose to believe I
do things and don't do them. Not always an answer, but
the feels. I shall continue to daydream.

# Poem 13

It doesn't matter if it's love and war
Mathematicians would argue or not?
I am no good at maths, but I observe
Cracking codes with and without the system
I see dreams and realities co-exist together
For all, it must be questionable to get here
Once you do, do it well.

# Poem 14

Every rejection might be your second chance
Freshly written scripts sometimes see no light
But does give you another door to knock
Knock as much as you can,
Might as well bang, but destiny has its plans.
If fate steps in and you lose everything you ever owned,
Destiny will save you in all hope.

# Poem 15

If I could write on petals, I would
I shall colour it purple and soft white,
Its fragile nature would remind me of the tender night,
The fireflies dancing on its edges, giving me light
Nature keeps me busy, and makes me forget city life.

# Poem 16

Writing while depending on artificial intelligence,
Is like using a catchphrase, editing it, and paying for its
maintenance.
Not using it will land you in the ditch of not trending
topics and leave you with a question.
Who does that?
The road not taken seems to be reconstructed, and I shall
prevent it with my midnights.
Help is help, but no more and no less.
We are here to be alive not end our own men.

# Poem 17

My entangled earphones are like snakes on a tree,
Providing shelter to my ears and camouflage to my
being.
Just like the invisible cloak, that frees my soul,
I can then sit anywhere and write, fulfilling my goal.
It's a different process for everyone, but the system is the
same
I try, I try, I try till I find my muse and my music does
not go in vain.

# Poem 18

Whether a quatrain or a long narrative poem,
I sit patiently reading different tongues.
I feel the scribbling before and the fine touch
My fingers press onto those words, when i'm moved too
much.
I bookmark making love to the torches, setting the pace,
I save some to read later, cause i am hiding my ace
I shan't say, the dreamers gotta learn the game.

# Poem 19

Bleed on paper, hands stained in red,
My heart is hurt, my brain is wrecked
Nobody around me, these midnights have no end
I am born again, with each poem in my head.

# Poem 20

The mirror reads 'You deserve it' in red lip shade,
I cross-verify by applying it in a classy way.
Tight, well put bun, with an empty wine glass in my
hand,
I don't drink, but I like to remind myself, 'You deserve it
anyway.'

# Poem 21

Why do you want to be a writer?
No reason, just like why would you pick up graphite
instead of ink to hit the white paper?
I don't feel the need to explain my canvas anymore,
I paint my language, I paint my shadows, I paint my
door.